Unso

Ghosts of Flight 401

Brian Innes

RAINTREE
STECK-VAUGHN
PUBLISHERS

A Harcourt Company

Austin · New York
www.steck-vaughn.com

Developed by Brown Partworks
Editor: Lindsey Lowe
Designer: Joan Curtis

Raintree Steck-Vaughn Publishers Staff
Project Manager: Joyce Spicer
Editor: Pam Wells

Library of Congress Cataloging-in-Publication Data
Innes, Brian.
   Ghosts of Flight 401/by Brian Innes.
      p.   cm.—(Unsolved mysteries)
   Includes bibliographical references and index.
   ISBN 0-8172-5475-7 (Hardcover)
   ISBN 0-8172-4272-4 (Softcover)
   1. Ghosts—Juvenile literature. 2. Aircraft accidents—Miscellanea
—Juvenile literature.
   I. Title. II. Series: Innes, Brian. Unsolved mysteries.
BF1461.I55   1999
133.1—dc21
                                                98-17354
                                                   CIP
                                                   AC

Printed and bound in the United States
   3 4 5 6 7 8 9 0   WZ   02 01 00

Acknowledgments

Cover Ted Russell/The Image Bank; **Page 5:** Dan
Esgro/Image Bank; **Page 6:** UPI/Corbis-Bettmann;
Page 7: Quadrant Picture Library; **Page 8:** Museum
of Flight/Corbis; **Page 9:** UPI/Corbis-Bettmann;
Page 10: Tim Bieber/Image Bank; **Page 11:** Jim
Sugar Photography/Corbis; **Page 13:** UPI/Corbis;
Page 15: Dan Esgro/Corbis; **Page 16:** Museum of
Flight/Corbis; **Page 17:** Ted Kawalerski/Image
Bank; **Pages 18 and 19:** Quadrant Picture Library;
Page 21: Nigel Blythe/Robert Harding Picture
Library; **Page 22:** Paul Loven/Image Bank;
Page 25: Yann Arthus-Bertrand/Corbis;
Pages 27 and 28: Quadrant Picture Library;
Page 30: Kevin Fleming/Corbis; **Page 31:** UPI/
Corbis; **Page 32:** UPI/Corbis-Bettmann; **Page 34:**
Phil Schermeister/Corbis; **Page 35:** Austin J. Brown
/Aviation Picture Library; **Page 37:** Hulton Getty;
Page 38: National Archives/Corbis; **Pages 39, 40,
and 41:** Hulton Getty; **Page 42:** E. O. Hoppe/
Corbis; **Page 44:** Mary Evans Picture Library;
Page 45: Hulton-Deutsch Collection/ Corbis;
Page 46: Todd Gipstein/Corbis.

Contents

The Fatal Flight

In 1972, a plane took off on a routine flight to Miami. How were those on board to know that it would end in disaster?

The Eastern Airlines Flight 401 was the nonstop run from Kennedy International Airport (JFK), New York, to Miami International, Florida. In 1972, a dozen new planes had been delivered to Eastern Airlines, and another 38 had been ordered and were about to arrive.

These new planes were Tristar jets, Lockheed's L-1011 three-engined craft, fitted with Rolls-Royce engines. They were part of the new generation of jumbo jets, like the Boeing 747 and the Douglas DC-10. They were wide-bodied and could carry more than 250 passengers at a time. Each new plane had cost between 15 and 20 million dollars. "The quietest, cleanest plane in the skies," was how one airline executive had described the L-1011. The new planes were the pride of the company, which nicknamed them the "Whisperliners."

PREDICTING DISASTER

On December 29, 1972, the plane due to fly Flight 401 was one of the new Tristars, number 310 (#310). The plane had been delivered some four months earlier, and it had already put in nearly 1,000 hours of flying time on other routes.

A wide-bodied passenger plane being prepared for flight (opposite). Preflight checks were all clear on the night that Flight 401 took off for Miami.

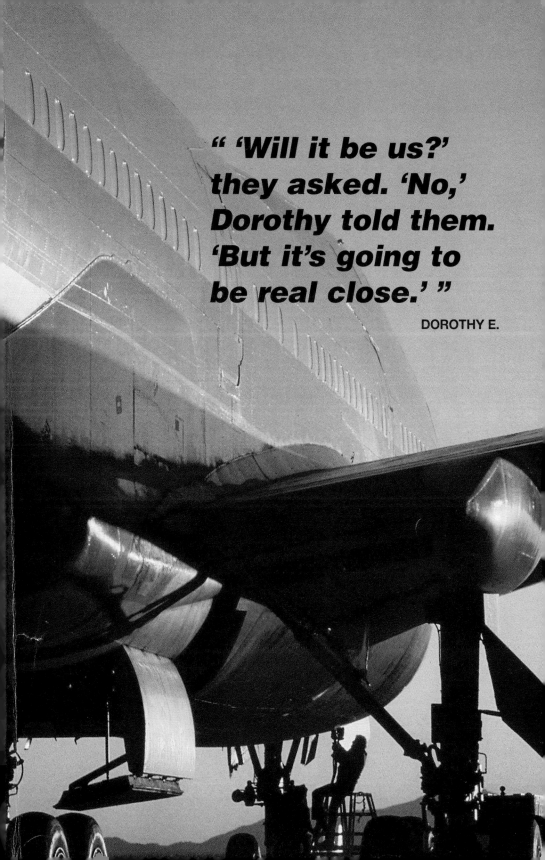

" 'Will it be us?' they asked. 'No,' Dorothy told them. 'But it's going to be real close.' "

DOROTHY E.

That day, #310 flew from Tampa, Florida, to New York. Among the cabin crew on that flight was Dorothy E. This is not her real name, but many of the people involved in this story asked that their names be kept secret.

On December 24, 1963, New York International Airport was renamed JFK Airport in honor of President John F. Kennedy. The President had been assassinated a month earlier. Here, Senator Edward Kennedy and his sister Jean Smith attend the renaming ceremony.

TERRIBLE VISION

Some time around the middle of December, Dorothy had experienced a disturbing vision. On a flight from JFK to Orlando, Florida, she had been suddenly overcome by a "weird, sick feeling." She imagined that she had "seen" a Tristar L-1011 over the Everglades, on its approach to Miami airport. It was dark and the plane's landing lights were switched on. Then the left wing seemed to break up, and the plane fell to the ground. Dorothy said she "heard" the screams of the injured passengers.

This experience seemed so real to Dorothy that she had to sit down to recover from it. She had experienced visions before, and they had come true. Two other flight attendants came to see what was wrong. Dorothy told them. They asked her if she knew when the crash was likely to happen. "Around the holidays," Dorothy said. "Closer to New Year's." Naturally, her coworkers were very worried. "Will it be us?" they asked. "No," Dorothy told them. "But it's going to be real close."

A NARROW ESCAPE

By December 29, Dorothy had almost forgotten her fears. The holiday period was nearly over, and she was due to leave Tristar #310 as soon as it reached New York. There, the cabin crew was to be replaced by another crew coming in to JFK from Miami on Flight 26. Dorothy was scheduled to return to Miami, via Fort Lauderdale, aboard another make of plane on Flight 477.

At about 7:30 P.M., #310 landed at JFK. The turnaround was 90 minutes, and the plane was due to leave on Flight 401 at 9:00 P.M. But Flight 26 was delayed, and it looked as if the replacement cabin crew would not arrive in time. Dorothy's fears returned when she was told that her crew would have to fly on Flight 401, instead of Flight 477.

It was nearly 8:40 P.M. when Flight 26 landed. The cabin crew hurried over to #310, and there was a

Lockheed's new Tristars could carry more than 250 passengers and in much greater comfort than on older aircraft. Unfortunately, in the event of a disaster, the potential for loss of life was also much greater.

Dorothy E. was relieved to see her replacement crew arrive on Flight 26 from Miami. This meant that she would not have to fly on Flight 401 after all.

last-minute switching of the two crews. The preflight checks were carried out, and the plane was ready for takeoff only a few minutes after the scheduled time. Relieved, Dorothy and her friends left to report for duty on Flight 477.

THE FATAL FLIGHT

All members of the cockpit crew aboard Flight 401 were highly experienced. Indeed, Captain Bob Loft had logged some 30,000 hours flying time, nearly 300 of those in the new L-1011s. His copilot, Bert Stockstill, was also familiar with the new plane. Second Officer Don Repo was an experienced flight engineer who knew every detail of the L-1011. All three were rested and alert. They had flown for only two out of the past 24 hours, from Florida to JFK.

Holiday air traffic was heavy, and Flight 401 was held up slightly at the end of the runway. However, the plane was airborne by 9:20 P.M. With the wind behind them, Captain Loft expected to make up the lost time and land at Miami International by 11:32 P.M. There were 163 passengers, the flight crew of three, and ten cabin crew aboard the plane.

Just before 11:30 P.M., the plane came within sight of the bright lights of Miami, to the south. Below, the blackness of the Everglades stretched away in all directions. Bob Loft checked with Miami Approach Control, then told Bert Stockstill to go ahead and lower the landing gear.

RAPID DESCENT

Don Repo kept an eye on his control panel, while Stockstill counted the rate of descent: "3,500 feet [1,068 m], 3,000 feet [915 m]. . . ." Then, Captain Loft suddenly noticed that one of the lights on his control panel was not lit. If the nose landing wheel was down correctly, this light should have been on.

The plane was now at 1,500 feet (458 m), and still descending. Loft called the Miami control tower.

From left to right: Captain Bob Loft; Copilot Bert Stockstill; and Second Officer Don Repo. These photographs were taken shortly before the terrible Flight 401 to Miami.

This is what the control tower of a busy international airport looks like at night. When the landing wheels failed to lower for landing at Miami, Captain Bob Loft asked the Miami control tower for instructions. He was told to climb higher.

"We're gonna have to circle," he told them. He was instructed to climb to 2,000 feet (610 m), and come around in order to try the landing again.

Suspecting that the panel lightbulb had failed, Loft and Stockstill tried to replace it. It would not come out. Repo left his seat and climbed down into the nosewheel bay to see if he could spot any problem. While all this was going on, nobody noticed that Flight 401 had not kept to 2,000 feet (610 m). It was steadily dropping toward the Everglades.

DISASTER STRIKES

At 11:42 P.M., the plane was at only 600 feet (183 m). It was losing height fast—at more than 25 feet (8 m) per second. But there was nothing to be seen in the blackness beyond the plane's window. Miami Approach Control ordered Stockstill to turn left. He turned the wheel. The left wing dipped down. A few

10

seconds later, it struck the ground. There was a burst of orange flame, a cloud of black smoke—then darkness closed again over the swamps of the Everglades.

There was a brief, terrible silence. Then came the cries and screams of the injured.

WHAT HAPPENED?

Every modern plane is fitted with a "black box" flight recorder, which is run by computers. It automatically keeps track of all the control-panel information during a flight. The flight recorder from Tristar #310 was recovered from the wreckage after the crash. It soon explained what had happened.

By day, it is easy to lose your way in the marshy ground of the Everglades. By night, it becomes almost impossible to know where you are. Until the ground came up to meet them, the crew of Flight 401 had no idea that they were seconds away from disaster.

As the plane circled above the Everglades, it was switched to autopilot. This is a device that steers the aircraft automatically. But for safety reasons, autopilot can be disconnected by a pressure of 15 to 20 lbs. (7 to 9 kg) on the steering column. This is so that the captain can take control again in an emergency. While he was leaning across to help Stockstill with the lightbulb, Captain Loft must have pressed on the steering column. He did not notice that the autopilot altitude, or height, indicator light had gone off. A soft warning chime should have sounded as the plane fell below 1,500 feet (458 m). However, the warning device was beside Repo's instrument panel, and Repo was in the nosewheel bay. And, because it was dark above the blackness of the Everglades, the cabin crew would not have noticed the ground rapidly coming up toward them.

"When he looked again for Flight 401's trace, it had vanished from his screen."

At a speed of 250 miles per hour (mph) (402 kilometers per hour [kmph]), with its left wing down, the "Whisperliner" crashed into the swamp. It broke up at once, flinging passengers—many still strapped to their seats—out into the mud and water. The giant engines broke away, sending up huge clouds of steam.

RESCUE OPERATION

In the radar room of the Miami control tower, the controller was puzzled when his scanner showed Flight 401 at a height of only 900 feet (275 m). Mistakenly, he had assumed that the trouble with the landing gear had been solved—and anyway, he had other planes to deal with. When he looked again for Flight 401's trace, it had vanished from his screen.

At 12:15 A.M., two rescue helicopters spotted a flickering light in the swamps below them. It came from the airboat of a frog fisherman. He was the first to the scene of the crash and was desperately trying to drag injured people from the muddy water. One helicopter landed on a levee, or embankment, some 500 feet (153 m) from the crash. The pilot radioed for help. Rescue vehicles would have to drive along the levee, which was some 8 miles (13 km) from the nearest road. The other helicopter dropped off two men. One was a medic. In the darkness, with only flashlights to guide them, the two men and the fisherman tried to rescue as many people as they could.

Of the 176 people aboard Flight 401, 77 survivors were eventually flown to hospitals in Miami. Bob Loft and Bert Stockstill died from their injuries while they were still in the shattered plane. Don Repo survived the crash, but died in the hospital.

When Flight 477 landed at Fort Lauderdale, Dorothy E. heard the news of the crash. The memory of her prediction came flooding back to her. But that was only the first of many strange events connected with the crash of Flight 401.

Rescue workers struggle to carry a survivor of the crash to an air ambulance. The darkness and the wet mud of the Everglades made the rescue operation an extremely difficult task.

The Pilots Reappear

After the crash of Flight 401, the crew of other planes began to experience unusual events.

There are thousands of indicator lights, dials, and switches in the cockpit of a modern jumbo jet (opposite). After the crash of Flight 401, many pilots claim to have seen Don Repo as they went through their preflight checks.

After the terrible crash in 1972, the Flight 401 route from JFK to Miami was operated by other Tristar L-1011s. However, in the months after the crash, beginning in February 1973, several members of the cabin crew began to have strange experiences in the lower galley of "Whisperliner" #318.

FACE FROM THE PAST

At first, stewardesses reported feeling very cold—even though the galley thermometer showed that the temperature was normal. They also said that they felt frightened, without any good reason. Then, one day, flight attendant Virginia P. was waiting for the elevator to take her back up to the passenger deck from the galley, where she had been preparing meals for the passengers. Quite suddenly, she noticed something out of the corner of her eye. When she turned to look, she saw a hazy white cloud.

As Virginia watched, a face appeared in the cloud. She saw it quite clearly, "with dark hair, gray at the sides, and steel-rimmed glasses." It was the face of Don Repo, flight engineer from the crashed Flight 401.

14

"As Virginia watched, a face appeared. . . . It was the face of Don Repo. . . ."

The elevator arrived. Virginia staggered into it, shaking with fright. She was afraid to tell anyone of what she had seen, even her close friends. But a month or so later, she heard of an even more startling event aboard Tristar #318.

AN EXTRA PASSENGER

The plane was at Newark airport, ready to take off for Miami. The senior flight attendant was checking the number of passengers against her flight list. There was one passenger too many. She counted the passengers again, and found a uniformed Eastern Airlines captain sitting in one of the first-class seats.

The stewardess spoke to him, but the man stared silently ahead. She was joined by the flight supervisor, who also questioned the man. But he seemed to be unable to hear them. Other passengers were now

This is a passenger cabin aboard a Tristar L-1011. Many people claim to have seen a person who looked like Bob Loft sitting in a passenger seat in the year after his death. But then he disappeared before their eyes!

Air traffic controllers have to keep a careful eye on their screens as planes come in to land and prepare for takeoff. After a long search for the extra passenger aboard Tristar #318, the control tower cleared the plane for takeoff.

watching with interest. The pilot of the plane came from the flight deck. He leaned forward to speak to his fellow captain but suddenly stopped in his tracks, "It's Bob Loft!" he whispered.

Then something amazing happened. Before the eyes of everybody, the man vanished. One second he was there, and the next second he was not. The plane was searched from end to end, but the extra passenger could not be found. At last, after a long delay, the plane was cleared for takeoff. It carried a puzzled and disturbed group of passengers and crew.

MORE MYSTERIOUS EVENTS

Now that other people had seen something similar to her own experience, Virginia P. no longer felt so upset. But there were other stories to come.

Some time later, Virginia was aboard #318, on Flight 26 to New York. On the way, the plane started to roll slightly to the right. Then it leveled itself,

The view of a plane wing seen through one of the passenger windows. A man on board Tristar #318 was on a flight to Miami in 1973 when he saw something strange over the right wingtip.

before rolling to the right again. When the plane reached JFK, it was checked thoroughly for faults. Everything seemed to be in working order. After a few hours, it took off again as Flight 401 to Miami.

OTHER STRANGE SIGHTINGS

Soon after takeoff, #318 began to behave with the same slight rolling motion. Then, a man sitting in a window seat called to Virginia: "What's that over the wing?" he asked. Leaning down to look past him, Virginia saw a strange hazy mass hovering over the right wingtip. She described it as being "about the size of a large suitcase." It was glowing, and was definitely not a cloud. It moved with the plane. If it rose several feet above the wing, the plane flew level. However, whenever it settled down on the wing, the

18

plane rolled to the right. After watching for a minute or two, Virginia called the flight engineer. He said that it was a cloud formation and that it would soon disappear, but he was puzzled by its behavior.

Some time later, another passenger reported seeing the same glowing cloud over the left wing. The plane landed safely at Miami without further incident. Virginia was able to comfort herself with the thought that she had not been the only one to witness the strange phenomenon.

KEEPING RECORDS

Another stewardess, Ethel M., began to keep scribbled notes of sightings that she heard about. One of the vice presidents (V.P.) of Eastern Airlines had boarded an L–1011, which was to fly Flight 401 from JFK to Miami. He went aboard before any of the passengers. He, too, saw a uniformed flight captain sitting in a first-class seat. The V.P. said "Hello" to the man—and then he realized he was speaking to Bob Loft, who immediately vanished. Loft was also seen by two flight attendants and the captain on another occasion.

During 1973 and 1974 there were many unexplained events aboard Tristars. Flight attendant Ethel M. decided to keep a written record of anything unusual.

On yet another flight from JFK to Miami, one of the flight attendants was

19

making her usual preflight check. She opened an overhead locker in the first-class cabin and found herself staring into the face of Bob Loft. She had known him well. On another flight, as #318 was over the Everglades on its approach to Miami, a man's voice came over the public address system. It gave the usual announcement about putting carry-ons under the seats and fastening seat belts for landing—but none of the crew had made the announcement!

TALES FROM THE GALLEY

There were also many more sightings of Don Repo in the lower galley. A catering crew was bringing food aboard #318 one day. Suddenly they left the plane in confusion and refused to go aboard again. They said they had seen a flight engineer in the galley, and then he had vanished in front of their eyes.

"She opened a . . . locker . . . and found herself staring into the face of Bob Loft."

One flight attendant was preparing meals in the galley when she found that one of the ovens was not working properly. She reported it to the maintenance crew, and a flight engineer appeared and fixed it. Soon afterward, another flight engineer arrived. He was amazed to find that the oven had been repaired, because he was the only engineer on the plane.

Later, when the flight attendant was shown a picture of Don Repo, she recognized him as being the man who had fixed the oven in the galley.

Some pilots claimed to have seen Don Repo in the cockpit during their preflight checks. Was he trying to help prevent the chance of any further disasters?

Cabin crew were not the only people to see Don Repo. On a flight from Atlanta to Miami, the second officer was sitting at his place in the cockpit. He suddenly heard a loud knocking sound coming from the nose well below the flight deck. He left his seat, opened the trapdoor in the floor, and shined a flashlight into the compartment. It was empty. Then, as he turned to look back at the control panel, he saw a face he knew well—it was Repo.

GUARDIAN ANGEL

On another occasion, a flight engineer came onto the flight deck to make his preflight checks and found a man in an Eastern Airlines uniform sitting in his seat. With surprise he recognized him as Don Repo. He

21

said later that the figure had told him, "Don't worry about your preflight check, I've already done it." Then the figure vanished. Afterward, a captain on a flight from San Juan claimed that he had come face-to-face with Repo, who said: "There will never be another crash of an L-1011. We won't let it happen."

INCIDENT AT PHOENIX

During the summer months of 1973, Eastern Airlines rented out several of their L-1011 planes to Trans World Airlines, or TWA. One night, as one of these aircraft was landing in Phoenix, Arizona, a woman passenger suddenly began to scream uncontrollably. The cabin crew could not calm her. She became hysterical and finally had to be taken from the plane in an ambulance. Between her sobs, she managed to say that a man had suddenly appeared in the seat next to

The airport control tower at Phoenix, Arizona. A Tristar had landed there in 1973 with a hysterical woman aboard. She said that she had seen a man vanish from the seat beside her.

her and then vanished. On another flight, a TWA pilot and copilot were going through their preflight checks. They saw a man sitting behind them—then he, too, vanished before their eyes.

"WATCH OUT FOR FIRE!"

In February 1974, another strange event occurred. It was written about in a newsletter produced by the Flight Safety Foundation. One day that month, #318 flew from Palm Beach to JFK as Flight 191. It then flew as Flight 903 to Mexico City and Acapulco. During the flight, one of the flight attendants was in the lower galley preparing food. She clearly saw the face of Don Repo, apparently reflected in the glass of one of the oven doors.

"There will never be another crash of an L-1011. We won't let it happen."

SECOND OFFICER DON REPO

She quickly took the elevator to the passenger cabin and asked another flight attendant to come back down with her. The second attendant agreed that a man's face was visible. It was not a reflection of anything in the galley. The two women called the flight engineer. When he arrived, he found himself looking at the face of Don Repo, who spoke to him. "Watch out for fire on this plane," he said.

The plane arrived safely in Mexico City. But, when it was being prepared for the next stage of the flight to Acapulco, number 3 engine, on the right

23

wing, would not start. The flight was canceled, and another crew was flown out from Miami to take the plane back there for an engine replacement. Flying even an empty L-1011 with two engines is a tricky job, but the crew were sure they could manage it.

"Watch out for fire on this plane."

SECOND OFFICER DON REPO

The takeoff with the unbalanced engines—one in the tail and one on the left wing—had to be made with great care. The plane had reached a height of only 50 feet (15 m), just off the ground, when number 1 engine stalled. The captain immediately shut it down and pressed a button to release carbon dioxide gas into the engine. This was to prevent the engine from bursting into flames. With just a single engine, the captain had to continue climbing. He gently nursed the plane to 400 feet (122 m), so that he could circle the airport and make an emergency landing.

The plane was grounded at Mexico City, and two new engines were sent down from Miami. But when number 1 engine was taken apart and examined, no faults were found. Why it stalled remained a mystery.

A COVER-UP?

The stories of the appearances of Bob Loft and Don Repo spread rapidly among the crews of Eastern Airlines. Pilots and crew of other airlines talked about it, too. But the Eastern management denied that any of their people had written reports of such incidents.

Several flight attendants decided to take a look at the flight log of #318. But they were amazed and disturbed to find that pages had been removed from the log. These were the pages for all the dates when Bob Loft and Don Repo had appeared.

PLAYING SAFE

Odd stories began to come from the ground maintenance crews. They said that parts that had been taken from the crashed plane #310—undamaged electronic, navigation, and galley equipment—had been built into other planes. Then, during 1974, orders came to remove these parts and replace them with new ones. Oddest of all, the black box flight recorder from plane #318, which had made the emergency landing in Mexico City, had also been removed.

This is Mexico City airport. In February 1974, Tristar #318 was forced to make an emergency landing here after one of the engines had stalled.

25

John Fuller Investigates

Many people began to report seeing the ghosts of Flight 401. John G. Fuller decided to look into the matter.

In March 1974, a respected journalist named John G. Fuller heard rumors about the strange events that were connected with Flight 401. He decided to investigate further. He spoke to many flight crew members, and learned more about how salvaged parts from #310 had been built into #318. Two mechanics that he spoke to had strange stories to tell.

MECHANICAL MYSTERIES

One told how he had been working in the lower galley of Tristar #318. The fuel tanks were being filled, and all the electric power was switched off. That was a precaution that was always taken when fuel was being loaded. It was designed to prevent any danger of fire. Suddenly, the fan in the galley switched itself on. The mechanic asked the electrical foreman how this could have happened. The foreman agreed that there was no possible explanation.

The second mechanic told another story, about a third mechanic. He was working in the lower bay and needed his screwdriver. He had put it down somewhere, but did not know where. Annoyed, he had shrugged and flung

A Tristar flies off into the sunset (opposite). For months after the crash of Flight 401 in 1972, there was often an extra passenger on board!

26

"... John G. Fuller heard rumors about the strange events that were connected with Flight 401."

This picture shows the raised wing flap of a plane. Wing flaps are used to control the airflow over the wing. This helps the pilot to regulate the speed of the plane. Sometimes, undamaged parts from crashed or old planes are reused in other planes. This had happened with parts from #310.

his arms outward, with the palms of his hands facing upward. Then he felt something being slapped into his right hand. It was a screwdriver!

Another time, one of the mechanics was working on #318 when he found men removing one of the galley elevators. He asked why they were taking it out. Was anything wrong with the elevator? "No," replied one of the men. "This is one of the parts that came from the crack-up of Flight 401. There's a work order to remove it."

CONFIRMATION

The mechanic decided to check with the stock department. He discovered that any part that had come from Tristar #310 was being removed. This included all radio parts, even if they had been fully tested and found to be in perfect working order. He also received confirmation that the black box had been taken from #318 after the emergency landing it had made in Mexico City in February 1974.

John Fuller was puzzled. Then, he heard about two Eastern Airlines pilots named Rich Craig and Stan Chambers. These two pilots were interested in psychic matters. They were fascinated by anything to do with the mind and spiritual, nonphysical things. The two pilots had been involved with a group called the Spiritual Frontier in Miami.

CONTACTING DON REPO

Fuller met with Craig, Chambers, and their wives at the Chambers's home. They agreed to hold a psychic session in an attempt to contact the spirit of Don Repo. None of them had ever met Repo, or knew what he looked like. After some minutes, Stan Chambers spoke. "I get a clear picture of a man. Dark hair, some gray. His uniform is very clear." He described the man's sideburns.

"I feel a rush of water coming up to the plane. It's coming up fast. I feel fear."

MRS. CRAIG

Mrs. Craig said: "I get the impression I'm feeling pressure around the top of the head. Especially around the temple. There must have been head injuries. . . . He doesn't quite know what to do." Stan Chambers continued: "He is saying something about a small door. Could he be trapped there? . . . I see a

29

porthole, like a round window. . . . Everything looks normal. It's forward of the galley . . . He's got a light. A small light. It's cold down there. Is there a passageway? I see his flashlight."

Mrs. Craig joined in. "I'm looking down the shaft to a wheel . . . Also see light shimmer on something below. Looks like water . . . I feel a rush of water coming up to the plane. It's coming up fast. I feel fear. Terrible fear. He realizes what is happening." Mrs. Craig suddenly looked very distressed. Stan Chambers was also upset. "He's trapped down in this hole and can't get up. He sees or feels the nose strut starting to buckle, and spray coming up!"

REVISITING THE SITE

Discussing the session later, everyone agreed that contact had been made with Don Repo. They all thought that his previous "appearances" had been attempts to contact various aircraft crew members.

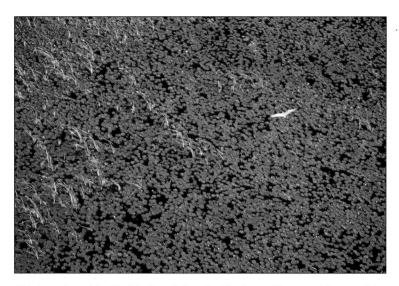

This is a view of the Florida Everglades. A white heron flies over this peaceful scene. Things were very different on the dark night of December 29, 1972.

This is the wreckage of #310 on Flight 401 to Miami. The photograph was taken the day after the crash. An inflated rescue raft lies in front of the torn wing section. Later, Fuller went back to the site. He took away a few pieces of remaining wreckage for examination.

One of the flight attendants John Fuller met during his investigations was Elizabeth Manzione. She joined him at the spot where plane #310, on Flight 401, had crashed into the Everglades in 1972. They wanted to see if they could find any remaining scraps of wreckage. They found about a dozen pieces.

EXAMINING THE WRECKAGE

These pieces of wreckage were taken to the Arthur Ford Academy in Miami. Students there took part in what is called "psychometry." Some people claim that if they hold an object, sensations and emotions connected with that object will come into their minds. However, Fuller felt that the results of this particular experiment were too vague. Some of the students spoke of plane crashes, fire, and a swamp

31

near an airport, but there were no details. After the experiment, eight of the students sat in a circle. Elizabeth Manzione sat with them.

After a few moments, one of the students said, "The baby lives." Then, Manzione spoke: "Her name is Christina. I get this name very clearly. There is also a Mrs. Jackson. A Mrs. E. Jackson . . . I also get the name Jacobs."

AMAZING FACTS

Manzione had never had an experience like this before. Later, when she talked with John Fuller, she swore that she had

This photograph was taken during the rescue operation in 1972. It shows a hospital attendant running to the emergency room with a two-month-old baby, who had survived the crash.

not seen the passenger list of the crashed plane. "Besides," she said, "I think there are two infants named Christina."

Fuller and Manzione looked at the lists of the dead and the survivors. There, among the survivors, was the name Christina Castado, aged two months. And, farther down, Christina Ochoe, one year old. In the list of the dead, they found Mrs. E. Jackson. And, among the newspaper clippings, they found the name of a man who had reported the crash—it was Jacobs! Amazed, Fuller and Manzione decided to carry out other similar mind experiments.

During one session, they began to receive messages from Don Repo. Fuller and Manzione asked: "What is your wife's first name?" The name they received was "Sassy." Perhaps this was a nickname. "What is the correct name?" they asked. "Alice," came the reply. Then Fuller received the name of one of Repo's daughters, Donna.

Elizabeth asked if there were any other messages. "To go phone Donna . . . Be good girl. P.S. I love her very much." And for his wife: "I love her . . . Tears don't help." There were more details about the crash, then two strange messages. "Did mice leave that family closet?" "To go into wastebasket . . . pennies sit there . . . boy's room."

A TASTELESS JOKE?

John and Elizabeth decided to meet with Mrs. Alice Repo and her daughter Donna. They had dinner together in Miami. Mrs. Repo told them of some other strange events that had happened in the months before the crash. One day, only minutes after she had spoken on the telephone to Don, an unknown man had called her. She had not recognized the voice. He had said that her husband had been killed in a plane disaster. Mrs. Repo said that she had not been worried. She knew that Don was on his way home from the airport. She decided that the telephone call was a tasteless joke.

STRANGE COINCIDENCE

Weeks later, on December 29, 1972, Mrs. Repo answered another telephone call. It was a man from the airport calling to arrange the crew roster for that day's Flight 401. Mrs. Repo realized, with horrible

The front and back of a United States Indian-head gold coin. When Fuller asked Mrs. Repo about coins, she explained that her husband collected Indian-head pennies. They are similar to these but much less valuable.

surprise, that it was the same voice that had earlier told her of her husband's death. Don even wondered whether he should take the trip, because it was not his regular shift. In the end, however, he decided to go. He went off to work, never to return.

MAKING SENSE OF THE MESSAGES

After they had talked for some time, John Fuller asked Mrs. Repo: "This might seem like a crazy question to you. Did you ever have trouble with mice in what you call your 'family closet'?"

"Mrs. Repo realized . . . it was the same voice that had . . . told of her husband's death."

Both Donna and her mother were startled. "How did you ever hear about that?" asked Mrs. Repo. Then Fuller asked about pennies in a wastebasket in

34

her son's room. "This is amazing," Alice said. "Don used to collect Indian-head pennies. There's a small barrel full of them in my son's room! But who told you all this?" John Fuller and Elizabeth Manzione explained about the psychic session. Alice was impressed and deeply moved, but she could not explain the name "Sassy." However, a few weeks later the last piece of the puzzle slipped into place.

Alice telephoned to say she had remembered the significance of "Sassy." At one time, she had put on a little weight. Don had joked about it. He had called her his "fat and sassy love."

THE END OF THE MATTER

Soon afterward, the hauntings of Tristars by Repo and Loft stopped. It was as if their souls had finally been laid to rest. Fuller went on to write about the story in his best-seller, *The Ghost of Flight 401*.

When Fuller contacted them, Eastern Airlines denied that they knew anything about ghost sightings. However, in addition to ordering the removal of all reused parts from Tristar #310, they also changed the colors of their planes. Was this, perhaps, an attempt to lay any ghosts to rest?

The Spirits of *R101*

After the crash of the airship R101, several people received messages from the dead crew.

The crash of plane #310 on Flight 401 is not the only air disaster that has been followed by ghostly sightings and "spirit messages." One of the most interesting cases concerns the giant British airship known as *R101*.

In the early 1900s, the Germans began to build airships. They were called zeppelins, after the man who first built them. They had a rigid framework covered with fabric. Inside were gas bags filled with hydrogen. The engines and cabins hung underneath the framework. One of these zeppelins was built for the United States, and it flew across the Atlantic Ocean in October 1924. It was called the *Los Angeles*.

UNHEALTHY COMPETITION

Airplanes that carried passengers could only fly distances of a few hundred miles in the 1920s. At that time, the countries that made up the British Empire were spread across the world, from Canada in the north, to Australia and New Zealand in the south. The British believed that airships such as the *Los Angeles* would be the best way of traveling around the Empire, so they decided to build their own airship.

In the 1920s, airships were thought to be the best way of traveling long distances. The Los Angeles was a great success. The R101 (opposite) was not so fortunate.

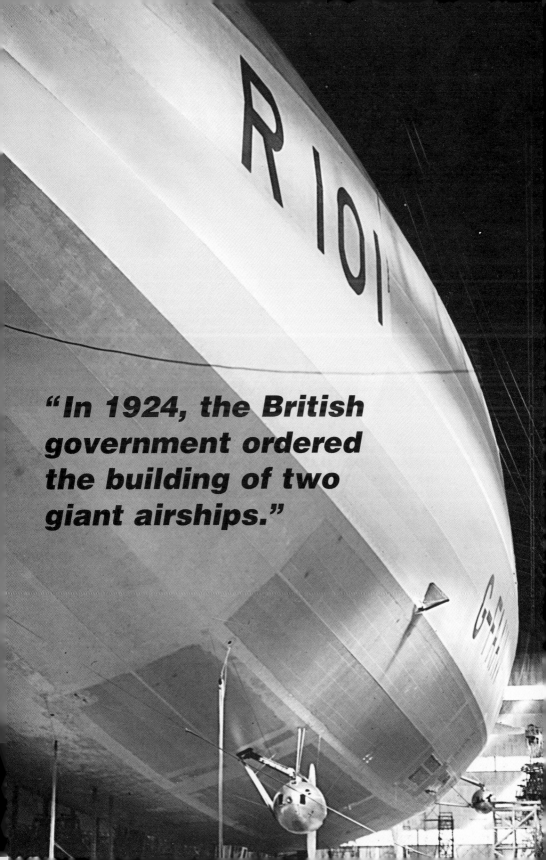

"In 1924, the British government ordered the building of two giant airships."

The American airship Los Angeles, *launched in 1924, had a long and successful career. This photograph shows it moored to the mast of a Navy ship, the USS* Patoka, *in the 1930s.*

Small, rigid airships had been flown by the British since 1917. They had all been given the letter R—for "rigid"—and a number. In 1924, the British government ordered the building of two giant airships. They were to be twice the size of the *Los Angeles*. Each was designed to hold 5 million cubic feet (140,000 million cubic meters) of hydrogen. *R100* was built by Vickers, a private company. *R101* was built by the national Royal Airship Works.

FALSE START

R100 was finished in 1929. It was able to carry 100 passengers. The design was successful. In July 1930, it crossed the Atlantic Ocean to Montreal, Canada, in 78 hours. However, the building of *R101* was a different story. When it was first tested in October 1929, a number of serious faults were discovered. Its framework and its engines were much too heavy. When it was loaded with fuel, crew, passengers, and spare parts, it could hardly rise off the ground. Even worse, the gas bags rubbed against the inside of the framework, causing leaks.

WORKING AGAINST TIME

Air Minister Thomson had planned that *R101* would fly him to India at the same time as *R100* flew to Canada. He said that *R101* had to be ready by October 1930. So the airship was quickly modified. The framework was cut in half, and another section was put in to make the airship longer. The inside of the framework was padded, in the hope that this would stop the gas bags from leaking. All this was done very quickly, and there was no time for testing.

Although it looks like a restaurant, this is the dining hall aboard the R100. *Up to 100 passengers traveled in style, enjoying all the luxuries of home.*

39

On Saturday October 4, 1930, at 6:30 P.M., *R101* set off on its first flight. There were 54 people aboard: the Air Minister and five other passengers, six men from the Royal Airship Works, five officers, and 37 crew. The weather was bad. It began to rain, and the wind was strong. At a height of never more than 1,000 feet (305 m), the great airship *R101* started its lumbering way southward into the wind.

BALL OF FIRE

Three hours after setting off, the airship crossed the English coast. It took two hours to cross the Channel to France. The rain was heavy, and the wind blew stronger. It drove the airship 20 miles (32 km) off course. Just after 2 A.M. on October 5, *R101* crashed into a hillside near the town of Beauvais in Picardy, in the north of France. The framework and gas bags split open, and the airship exploded in a huge fireball.

This photograph shows the huge size of R101. *It is moored to a mast next to Tower Bridge, London, ready for its first flight in October 1930.*

The framework of R101 *in a field near Beauvais. This skeleton was all that was left of the great airship after it had exploded in the early hours of the morning of October 5, 1930.*

The flames rose 300 feet (92 m) into the air. One man reported that it was as bright as day in the streets of Beauvais. Only eight men escaped from the blazing wreckage. Two later died in the hospital. The dead included Air Minister Thomson; Sefton Brancker, the Director of Civil Aviation; Major G. H. Scott of the Royal Airship Works; and the captain, Flight Lieutenant H. Carmichael Irwin.

UNUSUAL GATHERING

On Tuesday October 7, two days after the crash of *R101*, four people gathered in West London. They were there for reasons that had nothing to do with the airship. But they were soon to become deeply involved in the event. The place where they met was called the National Laboratory of Psychical Research.

It had been set up by a man named Harry Price. Price had been a friend of Sir Arthur Conan Doyle, the writer of the Sherlock Holmes detective stories. The two men had argued for years about spiritualism. They wondered whether people actually survived in some way after their bodies were dead.

DETECTIVE WORK

Conan Doyle believed that they did. He thought that people's spirits were freed from their earthly bodies and continued to exist once they were dead. When Conan Doyle died in 1930, Price decided to see if he could contact his spirit. He asked a famous psychic named Eileen Garrett to his laboratory, along with an Australian journalist named Ian Coster, and someone to keep a record of what happened.

The four people sat in the darkened room. Mrs. Garrett went into a trance. Then, she began to speak slowly in a deep voice. Psychics often claim that when they are in a trance they can receive messages from another person, whose voice speaks through them. This person is called their "control." Eileen Garrett's control was named "Uvani."

REASONS FOR THE DISASTER

Uvani told Price a few items of information about a dead German friend. Price knew that Eileen Garrett did not

Sir Arthur Conan Doyle in 1912. After his death in 1930, his friend Harry Price tried to contact him through a psychic. Instead, he received messages from the crew of the airship R101.

know this person. But there was no news of Conan Doyle. Then, Garrett suddenly became distressed. Tears poured down her cheeks. Uvani's voice said he had a name—it was either Irving or Irwin.

"The added middle section was entirely wrong. Too heavy . . . for . . . the engines."

UVANI, EILEEN GARRETT'S "CONTROL"

The voice changed completely. It began to speak in short phrases. The voice said that the airship was far too big for the power of its engines: "Engines too heavy. . . . Never reached cruising altitude [height]. Same in trials. Too short trials. . . . Weather bad for long flight. Fabric all waterlogged and ship's nose down. Impossible to rise. . . . The added middle section was entirely wrong. Too heavy . . . for the capacity [power] of the engines."

The three people in the room with Mrs. Garrett were amazed. Only brief news of the airship crash had been reported, and there were no technical details. Had the dead captain of the airship really contacted them through Mrs. Garrett?

MORE CONTACT

Three weeks later, Garrett was again involved in the mystery. This time, it was with Major Oliver Villiers. Villiers did not know Price and had not heard about events in the laboratory. However, he had been a friend of Sefton Brancker—in fact, he had driven him to the airship on the day it took off. He had also

43

known Flight Lieutenant Irwin. Late one night, soon after the crash, Major Villiers was alone. Suddenly, he "heard" Irwin cry out: "For goodness sake, let me talk to you. It's all so ghastly. I must speak to you. . . . Help me to speak with you."

Villiers heard about Eileen Garrett and at once arranged several meetings with her. The first session was held on October 31. It was different from the one held by Harry Price. This time Villiers was able to speak direct-

Eileen Garrett in a trance. She claimed to receive messages about the crash of R101.

ly with "Irwin," through Mrs. Garrett. Irwin's voice told Villiers: "We ought to have said 'No!' . . . The ship was too heavy. . . . During the afternoon before starting, I noticed the gas indicator was going up and down—which showed there was a leakage. . . . I told the chief engineer of this. I then knew we were almost doomed."

PREDICTING TROUBLE

Irwin then explained to Villiers how he had spoken with Major Scott and Squadron Leader Johnstone about the weather before they took off:

"The weather forecast was not good. But we decided we might cross the Channel and tie up at Le Bourget before the bad weather came. We three were absolutely scared stiff. And Scottie [Major Scott] said to us: 'Look here, we are in for it. But . . . let's smile like . . . Cheshire cats as we go on board, and leave England with a clean pair of heels.' "

At later meetings with Eileen Garrett, Villiers "spoke" with other members of the airship's dead crew, and with Sefton Brancker. He reported the content of all these conversations to the Court of Inquiry that was set up to look into the reason for the disaster. The Court would not believe the report.

ALL IN THE IMAGINATION?

So what are we to make of these strange stories? Did the ghosts of Flight 401 actually appear? Or were they just imagined by the people who thought they saw them? Did Stan Chambers, John Fuller, Elizabeth Manzione, and Eileen Garrett really communicate with the spirits of people who were dead?

Those who believe in spiritualism have no doubt. People's spirits live on, they say, after the death of their bodies. Spiritualists or psychics have a special ability that allows them to "get in touch" with these

Sefton Brancker (on the right), the British Director of Civil Aviation, died in the crash of R101. He later contacted Major Villiers through Eileen Garrett.

Many people have reported seeing ghostly figures such as this. Others claim to have received messages from the dead. Although researchers have put forward possible explanations for both, there is no scientific proof for these happenings.

spirits. Other people interested in psychic research have different theories. They believe in unexpected appearances after a crisis. Many people have reported "seeing" family members or friends just before they died, or at the moment of their death, even though they may have been hundreds of miles away.

Some researchers say that the intense emotions of the dying person are so strong that they produce a type of physical or electrical energy. This energy can be "seen" or "felt" by the people they were close to.

RESTING IN PEACE

Perhaps this also explains the appearances of ghosts. When people die suddenly, they leave many unfinished matters. Researchers have suggested that this causes great anxiety and because of this, perhaps, the spirit lingers on. Only after it has been reassured that everything is well with those who are left behind can it finally rest in peace. Then, the ghost is seen no more.

Glossary

assassinated To be killed by someone for political reasons.

coincidence A number of related events that happen by accident but seem to have been planned.

descent The act of going down.

flight log A detailed record of events during a plane's journey.

foreman An experienced worker in charge of other workers. Also, the spokesperson for a jury.

galley The kitchen on a ship or airplane. Also an oar-powered ship.

hysterical Wild, uncontrolled crying or laughter.

investigate To find out more information about something.

logged Officially recorded, or written down.

maintenance The act of keeping something in good working order.

modified Something that has been changed slightly.

navigation equipment Devices used to steer the course of a ship, plane, or other type of vehicle.

nosewheel Landing-gear wheel under the nose of an airplane.

phenomenon An unusual happening. Something that exists.

predicting Describing an event before it actually happens.

psychic A person who claims to be able to see into the future or who has other unexplained powers.

psychometry The unscientifically proven practice of holding an object and feeling sensations and emotions connected with that object come into the mind.

radar A device for locating objects, such as airplanes, using radio waves.

roster A list of people's names. Often used to schedule duties.

spiritualism The belief that the dead are able to send certain messages to the living.

stock department The department that keeps a record of goods stored in a warehouse.

tasteless In bad taste.

trance A sleeplike condition of the mind while a person is awake.

transmit To pass something on. Also to broadcast a radio, TV, or satellite program.

vague Indistinct, or unclear.

waterlogged Completely full of water, or totally soaked.

wreckage The remains of a wreck, such as that of a ship, plane, or car.

Index

Further Reading

Cohen, Daniel. *Dangerous Ghosts.* Putnam Publishing Group, 1996
———. *Ghosts of the Deep.* Putnam Publishing Group, 1993
Green, Carl R. and Sanford, William R. *Recalling Past Lives.* Enslow, 1993
Morpurgo, Michael, ed. *Ghostly Haunts.* Trafalgar, 1995
Powell, Jillian. *The Supernatural,* "Mysteries of . . ." series. Millbrook
  Press, 1996
Stacey, Tom. *The Hindenburg.* Lucent Books, 1990